- His palms are sweaty
- Knees weak, arms are heavy
- There's vomit

**VOICES IN HIP-HOP / EMINEM**

# VOICES IN HIP-HOP
## EMINEM

### AIDAN SIEGEL

CREATIVE EDUCATION / CREATIVE PAPERBACKS

...And since bi[rth I've been]
cursed with t[his curse to]
just cu[rse]

...And ju[st]
and bi[zarre]

...And it [...]

Published by Creative Education and Creative Paperbacks
P.O. Box 227, Mankato, Minnesota 56002
Creative Education and Creative Paperbacks are
imprints of The Creative Company
www.thecreativecompany.us

Design by Graham Morgan
Art direction by Blue Design (www.bluedes.com)

Images by Images by Getty Images/Aaron J. Thornton, 44, Catherine McGann, 39, Frederick M. Brown, 40, Gregory Bojorquez, 10, James Devaney, 32, Jeff Kravitz, 18–19, 22, Kevin Mazur, 2, Kevin.Mazur, 16, 28, Martin Philbey, 27, Michael Caulfield Archive, 36, Michel Linssen, 25, Nigel Crane, 23, Tim Mosenfelder, 9; Wikimedia Commons/Arthur Siegel, U.S. Office of War Information, 12, Mika-photography, cover, 3, 4, 15
Every effort has been made to contact copyright holders for material reproduced in this book. Any omissions will be rectified in subsequent printings if notice is given to the publisher.

Copyright © 2026 Creative Education, Creative Paperbacks
International copyright reserved in all countries.
No part of this book may be reproduced in any form
without written permission from the publisher.

Names: Siegel, Aidan, author.
Title: Eminem / by Aidan Siegel.
Description: Mankato, Minnesota : Creative Education and Creative Paperbacks, 2026. | Series: Voices in hip-hop | Includes index. | Audience: Ages 12–15 | Audience: Grades 7–9 | Summary: "Listen up! It's Eminem, the intense and provocative hip-hop artist. Part biography, part song lyric collection, this music-fueled title for high school readers celebrates the rapper's journey and voice. Includes a selected discography and index"– Provided by publisher.
Identifiers: LCCN 2024053927 (print) | LCCN 2024053928 (ebook) | ISBN 9798889892786 (library binding) | ISBN 9781682776445 (paperback) | ISBN 9798889893899 (ebook)
Subjects: LCSH: Eminem, 1972–Juvenile literature. | Rap musicians–United States–Biography–Juvenile literature.
Classification: LCC ML3930.E46 S54 2026  (print) | LCC ML3930.E46  (ebook) | DDC 782.421649092 [B]–dc23/eng/20241113
LC record available at https://lccn.loc.gov/2024053927
LC ebook record available at https://lccn.loc.gov/2024053928

Printed in India

th I've been
his curse to

t this berserk
— that works
nd it helps in

**VOICES IN HIP-HOP**

# contents

Foreword .................................................. 8

Introduction ............................................. 11

The Longest 8 Mile Race ........................... 13

Beginnings ............................................... 17

A First Taste of Fame ................................ 21

First Deal: *The Slim Shady LP* ................... 24

Game Changer ......................................... 26

No Slump: *The Marshall Mathers LP* .......... 30

The Show Goes On: *The Eminem Show* ..... 33

Pain into Power ........................................ 35

A Drought of Doubt .................................. 37

*Relapse* (the Album) ................................ 38

*Recovery* (the Album) ............................... 41

Later Career: The People's Champion ........ 45

Selected Works by Eminem ....................... 47

Index ....................................................... 48

**VOICES IN**
**HIP-HOP**

# Foreword

...

"I think he's the best MC ever. Point blank, period. Of course, there are going to be arguments about that because he's a White guy. I don't think anyone that's rapping can touch Eminem on that microphone."

—DR. DRE, IN A MARCH 2024 INTERVIEW ON *THIS LIFE OF MINE WITH JAMES CORDEN*

FOREWORD

VOICES IN
HIP-HOP

# Introduction

I'm as cold as the cold wind blows
When it snows and it's twenty below
Ask me why, man, I just don't know

—FROM "COLD WIND BLOWS" ON THE 2010 ALBUM *RECOVERY*

Eminem is an American rapper and hip-hop artist. He is the highest-selling musical artist of the 2000s. Eminem was the first recording artist to have 11 consecutive albums debut at number one on the Billboard 200 album chart. He has earned 15 Grammy Awards, as well as many American Music Awards, Billboard Music Awards, and an Academy Award for Best Original Song. Eminem is credited with popularizing hip-hop in Middle America and breaking racial barriers to the acceptance of white rappers in popular music. Through his passion, originality, and voice, he became a legend of hip-hop history.

**VOICES IN HIP-HOP**

Eminem's music is known for its fierce lyrical flow, bold intellect, and sense of humor. Although controversial at times, his honest, emotional, and original lyrical style has captivated fans all around the world. His reflections of self, family, friends, and life throughout his music are thought-provoking. They give his listeners a sense of comfort—the comfort that they are not alone when "the cold wind blows."

Detroit, Michigan

# The Longest 8 Mile Race

...

Eminem's legal name is Marshall Bruce Mathers III. He was born on October 17, 1972, in St. Joseph, Missouri. His father left the family when Eminem was a baby. Eminem has said in later interviews that he never met his father, who died before the two could reconcile.

As a child, Eminem was always on the move. His mother moved among several cities in Missouri before settling in Warren, a neighborhood in Detroit, with Eminem and his younger brother.

Warren, and the other Detroit neighborhoods where Eminem grew up, were poor. They were in a part of the city known as "8 Mile." 8 Mile Road is a highway that

**VOICES IN HIP-HOP**

runs through Detroit. It's known as the divider of the city and the suburbs, the poor and the rich.

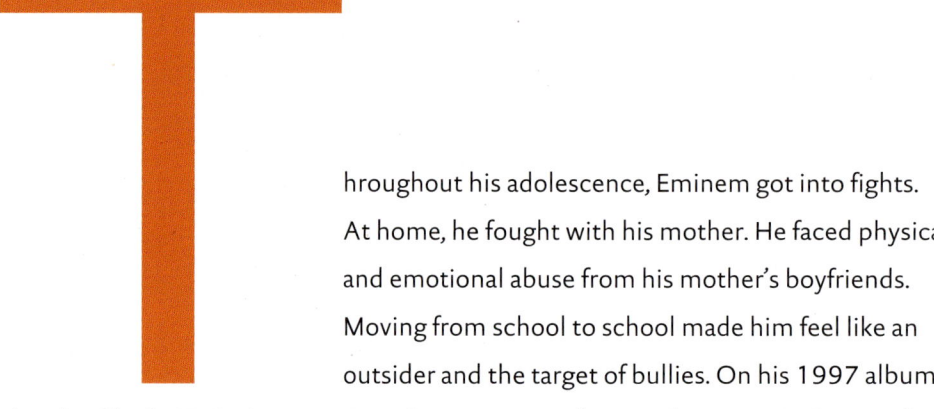

Throughout his adolescence, Eminem got into fights. At home, he fought with his mother. He faced physical and emotional abuse from his mother's boyfriends. Moving from school to school made him feel like an outsider and the target of bullies. On his 1997 album *The Slim Shady LP,* Eminem re-visits the memory and internal emotions of an incident with a bully in junior high school.

My first day in Junior High, this kid said
"It's you and I, three o'clock sharp, this afternoon you die"
I looked at my watch, it was 1:20
"I already gave you my lunch money
What more do you want from me?"
He said, "Don't try to run from me, you'll just make it worse"
My palms were sweaty, and I started to shake at first
Somethin' told me, "Try to fake a stomach ache, it works"

—FROM "BRAIN DAMAGE" ON THE 1999 ALBUM *THE SLIM SHADY LP*

VOICES IN
HIP-HOP

# Beginnings

The young Eminem wanted to tell stories. At first he wanted to be a comic book artist. But he changed his mind and turned to hip-hop after an uncle gifted him a rap soundtrack. When Eminem was 14 years old, he and a friend started rapping under the names "Manix" and "M&M." The name M&M later became "Eminem."

When Eminem was 15, he met runaway Kim Scott. Eminem's mother allowed Kim to stay at their home. Eminem and Kim started an on-again, off-again relationship. Kim would give birth to their daughter Hailie in 1995.

Eminem dropped out of school at age 17. He worked in low-wage jobs. He was a dishwasher and cook at a restaurant called Gilbert's Lodge. His first album, *Infinite*, released through Web Entertainment in 1996, failed to gain attention. It sold only 1,000 copies.

VOICES IN
HIP-HOP

The issues Eminem faced in his youth were part of the driving forces that helped him find his voice. He chose rapping as an outlet to express what he felt. His emotions translated into his lyrics.

### ANOTHER NAME

Eminem is sometimes called "the Detroit MC." "MC" or "emcee" stands for "master of ceremonies." In hip-hop, it refers to a skillful stage performer who can get the audience fired up. This use of the term dates back to the late 1970s, when rappers, for example, MC Hammer, often had the letters MC in front of their name. Before the launch of the Internet and digital music, these artists' success depended on their ability to perform live on the stage.

BEGINNINGS

…And since birth I've bee[n] cursed with this curse to just curse
…And just blu[r]

# A First Taste of Fame

...

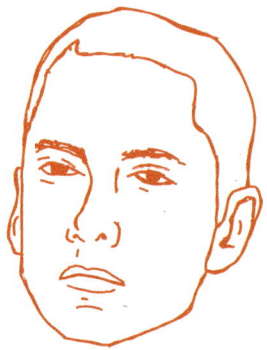

In the spring of 1997, Eminem recorded *Slim Shady EP*, an eight-song mixtape that introduced his fresh sound and his alter ego (other self) Slim Shady. A few months later, Eminem participated in the Rap Olympics in Los Angeles, California—the biggest rap and hip-hop competition in the world at that time. Prior to the competition, his personal life had begun to fall apart. He had lost his job at Gilbert's Lodge in late 1996. He had started abusing drugs around the same time. Kim left him and took their daughter with her. If anyone needed a break, it was Eminem.

Eminem went to the Rap Olympics with his then-manager and now long-term friend Paul Rosenberg. Rosenberg made sure the pair had copies of *Slim Shady EP*

**VOICES IN HIP-HOP**

on them so they could hand them out. Eminem's mixtape made its way around the event. Eventually a copy landed in the hands of Interscope Records founder and music executive pioneer Jimmy Iovine. Iovine listened through the unique flows and cadences of Slim Shady with none other than Dr. Dre, one of hip-hop's most influential, bold, and innovative figures. The rest is well-recorded history.

Eminem and Dr. Dre

A FIRST TASTE OF FAME

**VOICES IN HIP-HOP**

# First Deal: *The Slim Shady LP*

Eminem signed his first record deal in March 1998 with Dr. Dre's Aftermath Entertainment. On February 23, 1999, Eminem released the studio album *The Slim Shady LP*. The album debuted at number two on the Billboard 200. Fans and critics loved it. It's now certified quadruple platinum. It's one of the most successful albums released by Aftermath. The album earned Eminem the cover story in *Rolling Stone* magazine's April 1999 issue.

*Rolling Stone* writer Anthony Bozza stated: "In three short months, 24-year-old Marshall Bruce Mathers III has gone from white trash to white hot." It was a perfect description of Eminem at that time. His passionate, intense, honest lyrics and top-tier rap abilities were quickly the hottest new sound in the music world.

Eminem had drawn the attention of the public. Part of what made his sound so new and exciting was how bold he was. Eminem was showing everyone that he was not afraid to rap about controversial topics or make controversial statements, even when they were very inappropriate. He has been criticized for his violent themes and the slurs directed at women and gay people, for example. But no matter whom he would upset, Eminem wasn't going to sacrifice his voice.

FIRST DEAL: *THE SLIM SHADY LP*

**VOICES IN HIP-HOP**

# Game Changer

...

ntil *The Slim Shady LP*, hip-hop music was almost exclusively made of songs about growing up impoverished in the 'hood. Hip-hop music originated in The Bronx and Harlem. As hip-hop grew, several styles formed. The group Three 6 Mafia popularized the Memphis sound. A Tribe Called Quest was associated with the New York sound. Although the lyricism grew, the perspective was similar.

Eminem brought topics that an everyday, nine-to-five, average Joe could relate to. His angsty and fierce lyrics described bouts with mental illness, immense sadness, and

GAME CHANGER

Dr. Dre and Eminem

family destruction. He articulated emotions that everyone in some way goes through and is trying to figure out. Eminem's relatability reached a wider audience.

Hip-hop was created by Black people and performed in Black communities. It reflected their experiences. With his swagger and distinct personality, Eminem impressed the community of Black rappers who had birthed hip-hop culture. With his street roots and the honesty in his songs, Eminem wasn't looking to take anything from Black rappers. He just wanted to add to the greatness and beauty of hip-hop.

There were many reasons Eminem's career was impactful. Eminem's *The Slim Shady LP* started to break down the idea that a white rapper could not be successful without being a one-hit wonder. His music was not the type people had heard before. His rapping abilities were obvious when people heard the music. It was new, real, original hip-hop music.

## DR. DRE'S PRODIGY

Eminem's success proved Dr. Dre truly had an ear for talent and for developing artists into stars. Dr. Dre's connection to Eminem's music and image gave people inside and outside the industry a reason to respect Eminem, making him one of Dr. Dre's most successful prodigies. Eminem's several commercially successful albums and collaborations made the duo iconic. It solidified Dr. Dre's impressive understanding of talent. The pair made their impact on the genre forever, breaking records and making diamond selling ones. They made history by shaping an era of the sound and culture of hip-hop.

**VOICES IN
HIP-HOP**

# No Slump: *The Marshall Mathers LP*

....

In 2000, Eminem released *The Marshall Mathers LP,* one of the most commercially successful records not only in hip-hop history, but in all music history. In its first week, it sold 1.78 million copies. It debuted as the Billboard 200 number-one album for eight straight weeks. It's home to some of hip-hop's all-time hits, like "My Name Is" and "Stan." Now considered one of hip-hop's most legendary records, it has sold 25 million copies worldwide. It's 11 times certified diamond by the Recording Industry Association of America (RIAA).

With more chart-topping hits, the buzz around the Detroit native continued to explode. Eminem was becoming a global superstar and beginning a legacy. His music was original and real. He told stories through his unique point of view, yet he made them relatable to others. People could not get enough. The 8 Mile kid was becoming one of the world's next music icons.

And since birth I've been cursed with this curse to just curse
And just blurt this berserk and bizarre s— that works
And it sells and it helps in itself to relieve
All this tension, dispensin' these sentences

— **FROM "THE WAY I AM" ON THE 2000 ALBUM** *THE MARSHALL MATHERS LP*

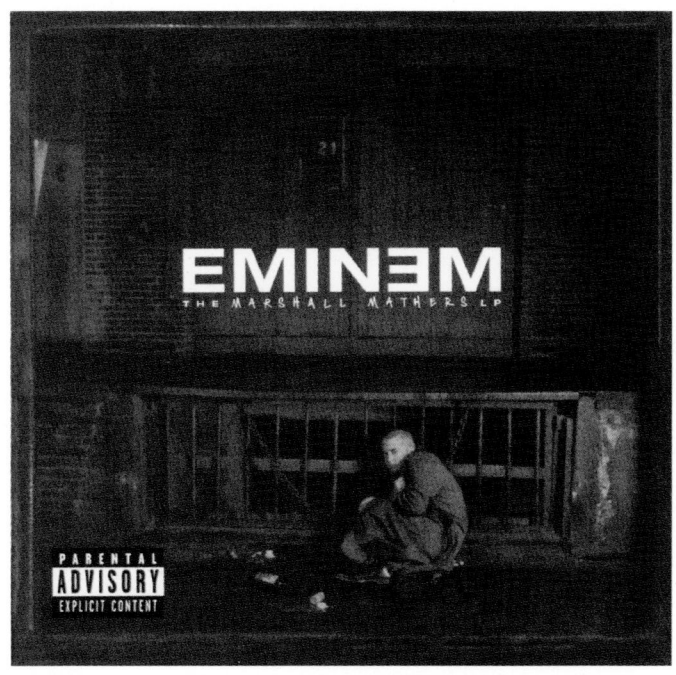

VOICES IN
HIP-HOP

# The Show Goes On: *The Eminem Show*

Eminem's fandom and superstardom continued to grow as he released his album *The Eminem Show*. The Detroit MC's 2002 record succeeded the acclaim of *The Marshall Mathers LP*. It sold 27 million copies and topped charts around the world. With hits like "Without Me" and "Till I Collapse," the album became Eminem's biggest commercial success. "Without Me" has appeared on the soundtracks of feature films like *Despicable Me* (2013) and *Suicide Squad* (2016). Part of what makes Eminem's legacy and cultural impact so monumental is the timelessness of his music. Years later, his music is still played and appreciated by fans of different ages, races, and religions. "Till I Collapse" still plays before high-school football games, for example.

The Eminem Show was not only a commercial success but also a personal triumph for Eminem. The media had created the narrative that he was only selling records because of his gimmicks. Some said his work would not have sold without his alter egos. Doubters suggested that the music was only selling because of its comedic aspect. Eminem shut these ideas down once and for all with The Eminem Show.

## ANGER MANAGEMENT

The Anger Management Tour was a rap and rock music tour started in the fall of 2000, after the release of Eminem's The Marshall Mathers LP. It included acts like DMX, 50 Cent, Ludacris, Snoop Dog, and more. It hosted some of Eminem's biggest and most historic live performances, in the prime of his career. The tour had several European legs and two shows in Japan. The final show of The Anger Management Tour was on May 13, 2005, at Comerica Park, the home of the Detroit Tigers Major League Baseball team.

In 2002, Eminem also released his feature film 8 Mile. The movie showed his struggles growing up in 8 Mile and his attempt to get out by becoming a rapper. It was a box-office success. The soundtrack released along with it sold 9 million copies worldwide and peaked at number one on the Billboard Hot 100 chart.

In the summer of 2002, Eminem promoted The Eminem Show on The Anger Management Tour. The tour went 32 shows across the United States and Canada between July 18 and September 8. All 32 shows sold out.

# Pain into Power

I'll get up 'fore I get down, run myself in the ground
'Fore I put some wack s— out
I'm tryna smack this one out the park, five-thousand mark
Y'all steady tryna drown a shark

**—FROM "WHEN THE MUSIC STOPS" ON THE 2002 ALBUM *THE EMINEM SHOW***

Eminem's music reflects his rollercoaster life. His reflection is done through creative storytelling about relatable situations. He talks about the struggles of everyday life, as well as the struggles of people on 8 Mile and places like it. He tells his underdog story.

Eminem uses his anger, struggle, and experiences from his darkest moments to make his music. He uses music as a form of therapy, a way to share his thoughts and emotions in honest form. One of his most interesting stories is about writing his song "Rock Bottom." He recalls in an April 2000 *Rolling Stone* interview that he had been fired from Gilbert's Lodge right before Christmas. He had so little money saved that he wasn't going to be able to get many gifts for his daughter. As he processed his pain, he made unique, head-bobbing hits.

While discussing relatable topics of parenthood, mental health, and addiction, Eminem helps listeners process adversity. His honesty and passion in tracks such as

**VOICES IN HIP-HOP**

"Lose Yourself"—his legendary ballad about believing in oneself and seizing the opportunity of hard work—give his listeners hope, enjoyment, and somebody to look up to. Eminem describes the artist-fan relationship in his hit "Stan." The song anticipates future obsession with celebrities and intense Internet followings. Eminem treats the topic with warmth and dark humor.

One of the biggest factors that has made Eminem an icon is the sound of his music. Almost all aspects of Eminem's songs are unique in their musical production and energy, not only to a listener but also to music production experts. Between his lyrics, cadence, rhythm, and language and dialect variations, he gives the listener a beautiful and intense orchestrated chaos.

> His soul's escaping through this hole that is gaping
> This world is mine for the taking, make me king
> As we move toward a new world order
> A normal life is boring, but superstardom's
> Close to post-mortem, it only grows harder

**—FROM "LOSE YOURSELF" ON THE 2002 ALBUM *THE EMINEM SHOW***

# A Drought of Doubt

It was my decision to get clean, I did it for me
Admittedly I probably did it subliminally for you
So I could come back a brand-new me, you helped see me through
And don't even realize what you did, believe me, you
I've been through the wringer

**—FROM "NOT AFRAID" ON THE 2010 ALBUM *RECOVERY***

After *The Eminem Show,* Eminem's career continued to grow. But as his fame grew, so did his addiction to prescription pills. He recalls taking up to 20 pills a day. He took prescription painkillers such as Valium, Ambien, and Vicodin. In 2009, he said, "Valium, Ambien, the numbers got so high I don't even know what I was taking." People around him at the time said he was not always very interested in making music once he got a certain type of high, and it was affecting how he was treating others.

Recorded at the height of his drug addiction in 2004, Eminem's fifth studio album *Encore* was considered his first flop. Eminem himself called it one of his worst projects. In 2005, Eminem checked into rehab for the first time.

**VOICES IN HIP-HOP**

# *Relapse* (the Album)

**D**uring the height of his drug abuse, Eminem took a five-year break from releasing music. Between the flop of *Encore*, his stints in rehab, and eventual recovery, there was no good time to create or release a new album. What he would come back with from his absence with was nothing short of excellence. Eminem's sixth studio album *Relapse* was a new show of maturity from the superstar—but still with the same intense, passionate swagger he always had.

The album is a deep dive into the Detroit MC's feelings and perspective after rehab. It recognizes his wrong turns. Eminem shows a new vulnerability and a new side of himself. In some ways the album makes his music even more relatable and impactful to fans. Eminem was back, and he was ready to climb to the top again. According to the International Federation of the Phonographic Industry (IFPI), the album was the best-selling of 2010. It has sold over 20 million copies worldwide. The real Slim Shady was standing up, proud. He was letting the world know he was back and meant business.

RELAPSE (THE ALBUM)

VOICES IN
HIP-HOP

# Recovery (the Album)

...

In 2010, Eminem made his full comeback with another new album, *Recovery*. This album was a huge success and put him back at the top of the rap game. It was another show of maturity in the evolving career and life of the super star. The album builds off of *Relapse* in a very artistic way. Many of the songs are about what he learned throughout addiction. But it has a much more positive and hopeful tone.

With songs like "Not Afraid" and "Love the Way You Lie" with Rihanna, Eminem relives the truth and relays the lessons he learned through his success. The album debuted as number one on the Billboard 200 and hit number one in 16 countries.

…It was my decision to get clean, I did it for me

…Admittedly I probably did

It became Eminem's third-selling studio album behind *Marshall Mathers LP* and *The Eminem Show*.

*Recovery* was a step of maturity musically, many listeners felt. Eminem was praised for turning his intense words and views into more meaningful, deeper messages. British journalist Neil McCormick wrote that it was "framing his misogyny, homophobia, and all-round bigotry with an undeniable sense of empathy and humanity." Some critics had mixed feelings about *Recovery*. They felt it that while it was mature at times, it was also shallow and self-serving. Kitty Empire of *The Guardian* wrote in her 2010 review, "His Recovery will never be complete—only a time machine can work that magic—but, in bursts, Eminem's health is very nearly rude."

## BACK TO THE ROOTS: BAD MEETS EVIL

One of Eminem's closest collaborators in the music industry is Royce da 5'9". Both Eminem and Royce are from Detroit. They met in New York after Royce had opened a show for Usher in 1997. The Detroit duo then formed Bad Meets Evil, first featuring themselves in a song of the same name, track 19 of *The Slim Shady LP*. Later that year, the duo dropped a double single with "Nuttin' to Do" and "Scary Movies." "Scary Movies" was featured in the 2000 film *Scary Movie* with Amanda Roberts. Eminem also featured on the second track of Royce's debut album Rock City. The duo separated in 2003 but came back together in 2011 to release an extended play titled *Hell: The Sequel.* The project was a success commercially and critically. It earned a number one spot on Billboard 200 for a several weeks and was a RIAA Gold record. It included hit songs like "Fast Lane" and "Lighters," featuring Bruno Mars.

VOICES IN
HIP-HOP

# Later Career: The People's Champion

As Eminem's career continues, he remains a living music legend. He has produced some of the highest-charting, highest-selling albums of all time. He sang some of the catchiest, most eyebrow-raising hip-hop anthems. He continued making music into the 2010s and beyond, with albums like *Revival* (2017), *Kamikaze* (2018), and *Music to Be Murdered By* (2020). While some of these albums received

**VOICES IN HIP-HOP**

mixed reviews, *Music to Be Murdered By*, especially, was commercially successful, debuting at number one on the Billboard 200.

On July 12, 2024, Eminem released his 12th studio album, *The Death of Slim Shady (Coup de Grâce)*. The album centers around a battle between Eminem and his alter ego Slim Shady, and how it has been viewed in society today. The album was his biggest commercial success since *The Marshall Mathers LP 2* (2013). It peaked at number one on the Billboard Hot 100 and was certified gold in Canada, New Zealand, Poland, and the United Kingdom.

Eminem remains relevant even after a long career. He connects with his fans, and he keeps close ties with the city of Detroit. He is an outspoken fan and supporter of the Detroit Lions football team. In 2024, he hosted the first night of the NFL Draft in Detroit, walking onto the stage to the sounds of his 2010 hit "Not Afraid."

Eminem has made his share of mistakes. He is a star, and his mistakes are public and receive extra criticism. But regardless of whether he is a bad guy or not, he wants people to know they are heard. He wants people know it's O.K. to be angry, and he wants people to know it's O.K. to go for it all. He is the living proof of the messages he spreads through his music.

Eminem is the people's champion. He is Marshall from Detroit, bouncing around 8 Mile home to home with his mom and his brother. He is the cook at Gilbert's Lodge. He is the skinny white boy impressing people at rap battles. He is Dr. Dre's prodigy. He is Slim Shady. He is Eminem, a legendary voice of hip-hop.

## SELECTED WORKS BY EMINEM

**EPS**
The Slim Shady EP, 1999

**MOVIES**
8 Mile, 2002

**TOURS**
The Anger Management Tour, 2000–2005

**SOUNDTRACKS**
8 Mile, 2002

**STUDIO ALBUMS**
The Death of Slim Shady (Coup de Grâce), 2024
The Marshall Mathers LP 2, 2013
Recovery, 2010
Relapse, 2009
Encore, 2004
The Eminem Show, 2002
The Marshall Mathers LP, 2000
The Slim Shady LP, 1999
Infinite, 1996

# INDEX

*8 Mile* (2002), 34
8 Mile Road, 13, 31, 34, 35, 46, 47
Academy Award for Best Original Song, 11
albums
    *Encore*, 37, 38, 47
    *Hell: The Sequel* (EP with Royce da 5'9"), 43
    *Infinite*, 17, 47
    *Kamikaze*, 45
    *Music to Be Murdered By*, 45–46
    *Recovery*, 11, 37, 41, 43, 47
    *Relapse*, 38, 41, 47
    *Revival*, 45
    *Slim Shady EP*, 21, 47
    *The Death of Slim Shady (Coup de Grâce)*, 46, 47
    *The Eminem Show*, 33, 34, 35, 36, 37, 43, 47
    *The Marshall Mathers LP 2*, 46, 47
    *The Marshall Mathers LP*, 30, 31, 33, 34, 43, 47
    *The Slim Shady LP*, 14, 24, 26, 29, 43, 47
alter ego (Slim Shady), 21, 34, 38, 46
American Music Awards, 11
Bad Meets Evil, 43
Billboard 200, 11, 24, 30, 41, 43, 46
Billboard Hot 100, 34, 46
Billboard Music Awards, 11
Bozza, Anthony, 25
Detroit Lions, 46
Dr. Dre, 8, 22, 24, 28, 29, 46
drug addiction, 21, 35, 37, 38, 41
Empire, Kitty, 43
Gilbert's Lodge, 17, 21, 35, 46
Grammy Awards, 11
Hailie (daughter), 17, 21, 35

Iovine, Jimmy, 22
Mathers III, Marshall Bruce (birth name), 13, 25, 46
McCormick, Neil, 43
nicknames (the Detroit MC, M&M, Manix), 17, 18
Rap Olympics, 21–22
Recording Industry Association of America (RIAA), 30, 43
Rihanna, 41
Royce da 5'9", 43
Scott, Kim, 17, 21
slurs, 25
songs
    "Brain Damage," 14
    "Cold Wind Blows," 11, 12
    "Fast Lane," 43
    "Lighters," 43
    "Lose Yourself," 36
    "Love the Way You Lie," 41
    "My Name Is," 30
    "Not Afraid," 37, 41, 42
    "Nuttin' to Do," 43
    "Rock Bottom," 35
    "Scary Movies," 43
    "Stan," 30, 36
    "The Way I Am," 31
    "Till I Collapse," 33, 34
    "When The Music Stops," 35
    "Without Me," 33
St. Joseph, Missouri, 13
*The Anger Management Tour*, 34, 47
violent themes, 25
Warren (neighborhood in Detroit, Michigan), 13